NASHVILLE

a photographic journey

photography and text by Bob Schatz

FARCOUNTRY
PRESS

I dedicate this book to my family, Lisa, Douglas, and Annie
without who's support and late dinners,
I could not have made all of these photographs.

I also want to thank all of my friends that helped
get me access to many of the locations in this book.

Finally I want to thank George Disario, Frank Siteman,
and Anne Brown, my muses.

—Bob Schatz

Right: The Japanese Garden at Cheekwood displays the colors of fall. Cheekwood is the former country estate of grocery magnate Leslie Cheek and his wife, Mabel Wood. Another Cheek family business was a coffee company whose roast was named after Nashville's most exclusive hotel, the Maxwell House. When visiting the hotel in 1920, Teddy Roosevelt exclaimed that the coffee was "good to the last drop."

Title page: Public Square Park in downtown hosts Live on the Green, featuring food trucks and music on Thursday evenings throughout the summer. Public Square Park is situated in front of the Metro Nashville and Davidson County Courthouse.

Front cover: Lights reflect in the Cumberland River as it flows below the Nashville skyline.

Back cover: Shomu-en, the Pine-Mist garden at Cheekwood, is a place of quiet and meditation. The pavilion frames a rolling hillside graced with stunted pines, maples, and flowering azaleas.

ISBN: 978-1-56037-700-9

© 2018 by Farcountry Press

Photography © 2018 by Bob Schatz
Text by Bob Schatz

For more information about our books, write Farcountry Press, P.O. Box 5630, Helena, MT 59604; call (800) 821-3874; or visit www.farcountrypress.com.

 Produced and printed in the United States of America.

22 21 20 19 18   1 2 3 4 5

FOREWORD

by Kathy Mattea

I first met Bob Schatz sometime around 1980, not long after I moved to Nashville. He was a good friend of one of my good friends, and our paths have intertwined at various gatherings over the decades.

He had a beautifully lit studio in a mid-19th-century warehouse on the Cumberland River downtown, where he was quietly building a successful busi-

"Warm, friendly, quirky, inviting, beautiful."

ness as a photographer, while I worked my way up through the music business and became a recording artist. Bob was not into photographing album covers and that sort of thing. His forte was something else entirely. He worked with scenes, moments, the essence of a place.

This book captures a glimpse of Nashville as she is today—but Bob and I both have watched her evolution over the decades.

When I started working my way through his photos, it was like watching my life pass before my eyes. I have spent time at nearly every single place in this book. I remember each of them, but somehow Bob captures a deeper experience—the energy of the place, the soul of it. The old meeting the new, the glow of the renaissance that is overtaking Nashville, and the celebration and sheer joy of having other people realize something we've all known for many years: that Nashville is a unique and wonderful community, and a fantastic place to visit. Warm, friendly, quirky, inviting, beautiful.

Whether you live here or you're here for a visit, picking this beautiful book up as a memento or buying it for a friend, Bob provides a look at Music City through a loving and respectful eye. The eye of a master.

Above: The Recording Angel at the Schermerhorn Symphony Center has blessed the Nashville Symphony with multiple Grammy Awards for their numerous recordings.

Facing page: Kathy Mattea warms up in the dressing room before her performance at the Grand Ole Opry. The Opry offers a package that allows you to witness scenes like this backstage.

Above: George Gruhn, owner of Gruhn Guitars, is one of the country's most knowledgeable experts on vintage American guitars.

Right: Since 1970, Gruhn's clientele has included Eric Clapton, Neil Young, Johnny Cash, George Harrison, Lyle Lovett, Vince Gill, Paul McCartney, and many other musicians.

Above: A Church Street wall features a mural by Australian artist Tyrone Wright, aka Rone, a fixture of Melbourne's street art scene. Brian Greif and Eva Boros began the Nashville Walls Project to bring international wall artists to Nashville. The Arts and Business Council of Nashville helps fund the wall mural project throughout the city.

Left: Street musicians follow in the footsteps of all the country greats by getting their start on the streets around Historic Broadway and the Ryman Auditorium. This musician performs in front of the mural at Legends Corner, which depicts some of country music's biggest stars.

Above: Every spring, over 800 cherry trees blossom throughout the city. Nashville has a special connection with Japan. Its consulate is located here, along with a large number of Japanese corporations.

Right: Belmont Mansion was built in 1850 by Adelicia Acklen, the richest woman in America at that time. During the Civil War, she and a cousin traveled through enemy lines to sell a fortune in cotton before the port of New Orleans was closed. Many of the gazebos and statuary that graced her gardens are now a treasured part of Belmont University's campus. The mansion has been restored to its former glory and houses a large collection of original furnishings and artwork.

Above: At the entrance to the Schermerhorn Symphony Center is a fountain featuring *The Birth of Apollo*, a bronze by sculptor Casey Eskridge.

Left: The Nashville skyline is connected to Riverfront Park East by the John Seigenthaler Pedestrian Bridge. Built in the 1980s, Riverfront Park commemorates Nashville's history of settlers by the Cumberland River.

Right: Hatch Show Print, across from the Music City Center, became famous when they began to print posters for many Opry stars, as well as for P. T. Barnum and Airstream trailers.

Far right: Music City Center spans three blocks and hosts some of the largest conventions in the country.

Below: A block from the popular honky-tonks on Broadway and across the street from the Music City Walk of Fame Park, the Country Music Hall of Fame and Museum adds a strikingly modern touch to the Nashville skyline.

These pages: The Cathedral of the Incarnation was dedicated in 1914, but renovated in 1937 because the congregation thought it was too dark. Ornate details decorate the cathedral—some serving other purposes like the porthole above with a view of the alter, used by the choirmaster to take his cues during the service.

Right: Historic Broadway is lined with honky-tonks including Tootsie's Orchid Lounge, Legends Corner, Second Fiddle, The Stage, and Robert's Western World, among others.

Below: A bachelorette party pedals down the street in the Historic Broadway District. Nashville was recently ranked as the "#1 Girlfriend Getaway" by *Travel + Leisure* magazine.

Above: Completed in 1851, Downtown Presbyterian Church is considered one of the finest examples of Egyptian Revival architecture in the nation. Wall murals painted to look like the Egyptian temple at Luxor and the stained-glass windows give a feeling of a desert oasis.

Facing page: A full-scale reproduction of the Parthenon was the centerpiece to the Tennessee Centennial Exposition of 1897. So loved by the city, the Parthenon was rebuilt as a permanent feature of Centennial Park in the 1920s. In 1982, the city commissioned Nashville sculptor Alan LeQuire to complete the Parthenon with an original replica of Athena Parthenos, now the largest indoor sculpture in North America. Athena holds Nike in one hand and her shield in the other.

Right: Commemorating World War I, Nashville native Belle Kinney sculpted *Victory* in 1925 for the War Memorial Plaza.

Far right: Every hour, this 95-bell carillon plays a reminder of Tennessee's musical heritage at the Bicentennial Capitol Mall State Park. The bells represent the citizens of the ninety-five counties in the state, and a 96th bell, located on the grounds of the Tennessee State Capitol, answers as a symbol of how government should answer to the people.

Below: The World War II Memorial within Bicentennial Capitol Mall features an 18,000-pound black granite globe that floats on one-eighth inch of water. It shows the different theaters where Tennesseans fought in the war. On either side of the globe are columns depicting the war's major battles.

Left: The Nashville Sounds, AAA Affiliate of the Oakland Athletics, take the baseball field at the bottom of the inning.

Far left: First Tennessee Park is the home of the Nashville Sounds. The downtown location makes a dramatic backdrop for the ballpark's historic guitar-shaped scoreboard.

Below: Nashville may be most known as Music City, but local hockey fans call it "Smashville" for the city's beloved National Hockey League franchise, The Nashville Predators. Named after bones of a saber-toothed tiger found in the area, the Predators went all the way to the seventh game of the Stanley Cup Finals in 2016-2017.

Above: The Schermerhorn Symphony Center hosts a range of concerts, which have included Buddy Guy, Sheryl Crow, Diana Ross, Tony Bennett, John Williams, and other great musical talents.

Right: The Nashville Symphony is led by Grammy Award-winning conductor and music director Giancarlo Guerrero.

Far right: The Schermerhorn Symphony Center is named for the former longtime conductor of the Nashville Symphony, Kenneth Schermerhorn, and is widely considered one of the world's finest acoustical venues.

Above: Rosanne Cash, artist-in-residence at the Country Music Hall of Fame, performs with Lucinda Williams and Emmy Lou Harris in the CMA Theater.

Left: Ricky Skaggs and Kentucky Thunder perform at the Ryman Auditorium. The Ryman is known as the "Mother Church of Country Music" and was home to the Grand Ole Opry from 1943–1974. Today, it is considered by many to be Nashville's favorite music venue.

Above: Cheekwood Estate and Gardens was built by Leslie Cheek and Mabel Wood in 1929, toward the end of the era of great American country estates. It is now home to a large fine arts and decorative arts collection along with fifty-five acres of botanical gardens.

Right: The Swan Fountain sits in the middle of the back lawn and is the centerpiece of Cheekwood's annual Swan Ball, Nashville's premier white tie charity gala.

Far right: One of Cheekwood's many water features is frozen in a winter snow. The house and gardens were both designed by architect Bryant Fleming.

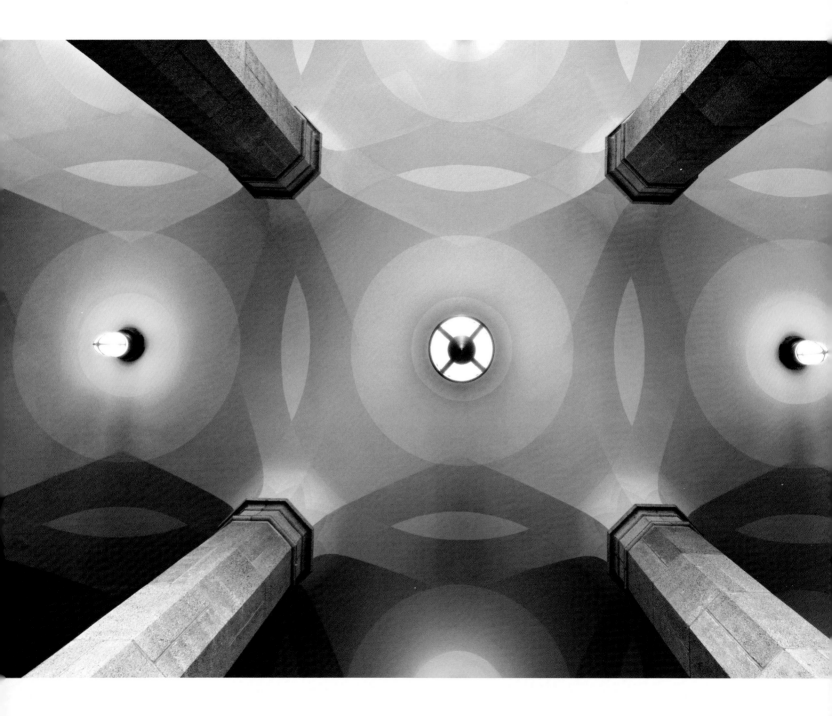

Above: This bell tower is a landmark recently built on the campus of Tennessee State University as a visual draw to the Floyd-Payne Campus Center.

Left: Located to the south of Nashville, Williamson County is horse country—home to many breeders and trainers of champion quarter horses and Tennessee walking horses.

Far left: Fisk University's Kravath Hall is just one example of the rich art and architectural heritage on campus.

Right: Downtown Nashville's Riverfront Station is the western terminus for the Music City Star regional commuter train, which runs east to service Donelson, Mt. Juliet, Martha, and Lebanon.

Below: Three major interstates converge on Nashville like spokes on a wagon wheel, making Nashville a prime spot for business logistics. I-65, I-24, and I-40 come into downtown and loop around the core.

Left: East Nashville neighborhoods have been reinvented as some of the city's most desired, hip, new areas to live, play, and eat. Adjacent to downtown, the neighborhoods are easily walkable to parks, greenways, galleries, and music venues. East Nashville is a great place to escape without leaving the city and has attracted many musicians and visual artists.

Far left: Historic Belle Meade mansion, once the centerpiece of a 5,400-acre plantation, is a premier example of antebellum architecture in the United States. Widely known for its champion thoroughbred breeding program, Belle Meade was home to Iroquois, the famous racehorse and stud to a championship bloodline that included Triple Crown-winner Secretariat. Today, this magnificent estate is a thirty-acre historic site that features guided tours of its 1853 Greek Revival mansion.

Below: Leiper's Fork, a historic village just outside Nashville, is a homegrown mix of picturesque surroundings, culture, and Southern fare. Many of the surrounding farms are home to country music and movie stars such as Carrie Underwood, Keith Urban and Nicole Kidman, Wynona and Ashley Judd, and Alan Jackson.

Right: The Gaylord Opryland Resort is known for its nine acres of lush gardens under glass and metal skylights that are separated into three areas, the Cascades, the Delta, and the Garden Conservatory. Each of the three atriums offers a unique experience. Approximately 50,000 varieties of tropical plants, several waterfalls and waterways, and miles of scenic walkways combine for an enjoyable afternoon of exploration. Refuel and relax in any of the fifteen different restaurants.

Far right: Gaylord Opryland's "A Country Christmas" is a Nashville holiday tradition. The Gaylord Opryland Hotel, built in 1977 and expanded many times since, is next door to the legendary Grand Ole Opry House.

Below: The original lobby of the Gaylord Opryland Hotel, built to resemble a Southern mansion, is decked out for the holidays with a beautiful tree and festive garland decorating its grand staircase and cozy fireplaces.

Above: Centennial Park is located across West End Avenue from Vanderbilt University. The 132-acre park is home to the Parthenon, Centennial Arts Center, Dance Center, and Sportsplex. Thousands of visitors enjoy festivals and concerts throughout the year. *The Mars Molecule Project* sculpture by Mario Martinez is an example of the city's revolving outdoor arts program.

Facing page: Designed and built in 1845 by renowned architect William Strickland, the Tennessee State Capitol is the second-oldest state capitol still in use today. Strickland died in 1854 before its completion and was buried inside the wall of the capitol, his greatest work.

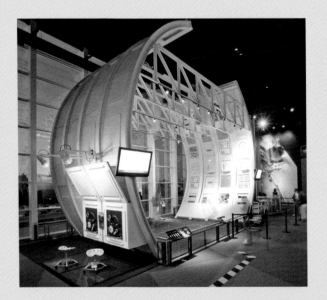

Above: The Adventure Science Center's exterior lights up with its iconic pyramid above the Sudekum Planetarium.

Right: The Moon Walker at the science center allows visitors to feel the one-sixth gravity of the moon's surface, while the adjacent EVA Experience offers the zero gravity experience of a spacewalk.

Far right: The sixty-three-foot dome of the Sudekum Planetarium is host to over twenty planetarium shows and more than fifteen laser light shows.

Above: Andrew Jackson's tomb was built for both himself and his wife, Rachel, after her sudden death, and was designed by architect David Morrison after a Greek temple found in the scenic wallpaper Rachel had chosen for the entrance hall to the Hermitage. The tomb was sited in her favorite place, the flower garden.

Left: The Hermitage, home to President Andrew Jackson, was built near his first home, Tulip Grove, in 1817. After a devastating fire in 1834, it was rebuilt and redesigned into the mansion that exists today.

Facing page: McGavock Mansion, also known as Two Rivers Mansion, is one of the earliest and best preserved of the early Italianate houses in Middle Tennessee, part of an 1,100-acre plantation. Its location between the Stones and Cumberland Rivers suggested the name given to the place by an early owner, William Harding. Built by David McGavock in 1859, the fourteen-acre tract includes the mansion and a small brick house built earlier, in 1802, and is listed on the National Register of Historic Places. It was purchased by the metropolitan government of Nashville and Davidson County in 1966 to be used as a park and events facility.

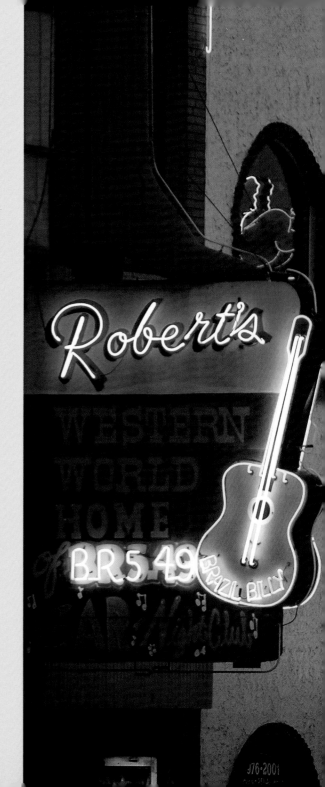

Above: Mr. Hats Boot Company is one of the newer neon signs lighting the Historic Broadway District.

Right: Both historic and new neon signs illuminate the crowded sidewalks of Lower Broadway.

Left: Originally designed to be ornamental rain gutters—their frightening appearance to ward off evil and as a reminder of eternal damnation—gargoyles, Latin for gullet or drain, watch over the exterior of downtown's Christ Church Cathedral.

Far left: Designed by New York architect Francis H. Kimball, the Victorian-Gothic style Christ Church Cathedral was built from 1887 to 1894, and officially became the Cathedral of the Diocese of Tennessee for the Episcopal Church in 1997.

Below: The Fisk Memorial Chapel is rich in intellectual and cultural history. Fisk University is a private, historically black university founded in 1866. Many religious and political leaders such as Martin Luther King Jr., Thurgood Marshall, and Jesse Jackson have spoken here. It has also been a venue for concerts by Duke Ellington, Louis Armstrong, W. C. Handy, and Nat King Cole, among others. The chapel was designed by William B. Bigelow of New York City and completed in 1892. It houses an extraordinary 40-rank Holtkamp pipe organ, one of the finest examples in the United States of the work of famed organ-builder Walter Holtkamp, Sr.

Above: Nashville's Arcade is the second-oldest shopping mall still in use in the United States. Milan's Galleria Vittorio Emanuele II, the world's oldest shopping mall, inspired its design. Almost a quarter of Nashville's population in 1903 came out for the grand opening.

Right: The Lane Motor Museum sports one of the largest European car collections in the country. Some are in showroom condition while others are being restored to near factory specifications to attain the museum's goal of maintaining every vehicle in running order. The museum is located in the Sunbeam Bakery, a well-known Nashville landmark.

Above: Historic signage on First Avenue South adds character to the neighborhood. This view is easily seen from the elevated vantage point of the Seigenthaler Pedestrian Bridge.

Left: Frist Center for the Arts has become a magnet for Nashville's rapidly expanding visual arts scene. The vision of the center is to inspire people through art to look at their world in new ways. This piece was part of the exhibit Secrets of Buddhist Art, organized by the Newark Museum.

Far left: Historic buildings, such as the Stahlman & Nashville Bank buildings, have been saved from demolition thanks to the efforts of preservation groups like Historic Nashville. Many have been repurposed into lofts, hotels, restaurants, and other uses.

Above: Korean Veterans Memorial Bridge arches over the Cumberland River. It was built as a replacement for the vehicular traffic on the John Seigenthaler Pedestrian Bridge—both bridges now link the East Nashville neighborhoods to the city center.

Right: State-of-the-art lighting and sound make Ascend Amphitheater a popular concert venue. Located on the Cumberland River in Nashville's SoBro district, the amphitheater is an easy walk from restaurants and hotels on Broadway and the rest of downtown.

Far right: Since its installation in 2007, the sculpture *Ghost Ballet for the East Bank Machineworks* has become a recognizable part of the Nashville skyline. Artist Alice Aycock honors the many factories and businesses that sat on the east bank of the Cumberland River and, in a way, the tornado that reshaped East Nashville.

Above: In 1850, Adelicia Acklen modeled the Belmont Mansion after an Italian summer villa called Bellemonte. During the occupation of Nashville, Adelicia invited the Union army to use Belmont as its headquarters. She used that connection to travel through Union lines and ship the last load of cotton out of New Orleans, making her the richest woman in America. Three months after the war, she left for Europe to claim her money—some of which she used to buy a number of marble statues for the mansion.

Left: Sited on the highest hill downtown, the Tennessee State Capitol was built in 1845 but not completed until 1859. Ornate cast-iron stairs and railings inside the capitol were home to the Tennessee State Library for over 100 years. Today, the former library space is a lounge for state senators and representatives.

Far left: Noted architect William Strickland designed the Roman arches that soar forty-two feet above the Grand Hall of the Tennessee State Capitol, framing the gilded chandelier hanging between the two legislative bodies.

Above: Legends Corner is one of the many honky-tonks playing live music every night along Historic Broadway. Historically, honky-tonks were rough establishments with music that served alcohol. Many performers who started out playing in these clubs went on to become country music stars.

Facing page: Writer's Night at the Bluebird Café is a must-have experience for locals and visitors alike. The famed cafe is the premier venue to hear up-and-coming singer/songwriters alongside industry veterans. Famous faces pop in regularly to play or catch a show. The cafe was made even more famous when it was featured as a regular location in the network television show Nashville.

Above: The CMA Music Festival is the foremost annual event of country music. Top performers and tens of thousands of country music fans from around the world flood Nashville's downtown streets and venues.

Right: The Boot Barn on Broadway sells the country-western lifestyle with cowboy hats, boots, and clothing. Vintage Hatch Show Print posters decorate the walls.

Above: The portrait of Adelicia Acklen looks down the grand staircase that leads into the ballroom of the Belmont Mansion, one of the few nineteenth-century homes whose history revolves around the life of a woman. Margaret Mitchell said Adelicia was one of the women she modeled Scarlett O'Hara after in her book *Gone with the Wind.*

Left: The Hermitage Hotel Veranda shows the attention to detail in this 1910 Beaux Arts beauty. Located across from the Tennessee State Capitol, the Hermitage has often been witness to history. In 1920, it was the headquarters of the women's suffrage movement as Tennessee ratified the 19th Amendment to give women nationwide the right to vote.

Facing page: Purchased in 1949, Far Hills Mansion became the Tennessee Executive Residence—so named because "Governor's Mansion" was thought to sound snooty. In 2002, Governor Phil Bredesen began six years of renovations to bring the mansion back to its former glory. Many distinguished guests—U.S. presidents, international royalty, and even Nashville's pop culture king, Elvis—have stayed here.

Left: The Ernest Tubb Record Shop is a one-stop shop for country and bluegrass CDs, DVDs, LPs, books, and memorabilia. It was founded by the legendary country music artist and Grand Ole Opry member Ernest Tubb in 1947. Tubb was later inducted into the Country Music Hall of Fame.

Far left: The Country Music Hall of Fame and Museum has been called the "Smithsonian of Country Music" for its extensive collection and recent $100 million expansion. With numerous interactive exhibits, artifacts and photographs, the permanent exhibit, *Sing Me Back Home*, allows fans and newcomers to explore the history and origins of country music. Older recordings and films are reengineered by skilled technicians to enhance the experience. Contemporary exhibits show why country music continues to increase in popularity.

Below: Bestselling author Ann Patchett and her partner, Karen Hayes, opened Parnassus Books in 2011, leading a revival in independent bookstores. In Greek mythology, Mount Parnassus was the home of literature, learning, and music, inspiring a fitting name for a bookstore in the "Athens of the South."

Right: The Nashville Zoo is home to this meerkat and 2,763 other animals, 365 species in total. Meerkats are great diggers and can excavate vast tunnel systems with many rooms, which not only provide protection from predators, but also keep them cool in the heat of African summers.

Far right: Located on the grounds of the Nashville Zoo, the 1815 Croft House at Grassmere is the second-oldest house open to the public in Davidson County. The Croft sisters donated their 180-acre family farm and home with the stipulation that they be preserved to educate Nashvillians about animals and the environment.

Below: In 1996, the Nashville Zoo moved from its original location in Cheatham County to Grassmere, six miles southeast of downtown Nashville.

Left: Chef Tandy Wilson had been a semifinalist nine times before winning the prestigious James Beard Award for Best Chef in the Southeast. He fuses his Southern roots with contemporary Italian cooking at City House, which has long been in the top echelon of Nashville restaurants. Nashville has been named one of "America's Best Cities for Foodies" by *Travel + Leisure.*

Facing page: The I Dream of Weenie food truck found a permanent spot in East Nashville's Five Points neighborhood before the food truck craze hit Nashville hard. Music City's food trucks offer an eclectic mix of diverse cuisine to satisfy everyone's culinary tastes.

Below: Nashville BBQ has emerged from the shadows of Memphis and is currently sitting atop many "best of" lists for barbeque. Martin's Bar-B-Que Joint, located in the Belmont neighborhood, helped make this happen. Martin's four whole hog pits contribute a hickory-smoked aroma that draws tourists and locals alike into this casual, full-service restaurant.

Above: John Graham conducts the soundtrack to the new *Final Fantasy* video game at Ocean Way Studio, located in the heart of Nashville's famous Music Row. Housed in a 100-year-old Gothic Revival grey-stone church with stained-glass windows, Ocean Way Nashville creates a unique atmosphere, large enough for orchestra, yet versatile enough to handle a single voice-over.

Right: Long before it was a historic hotel, Union Station was designed to dramatize America's economy and transportation. The high level of craftsmanship is shown in every detail, from the barrel-vaulted ceiling and Tiffany-style stained glass to the carved woodwork and gilded plaster reliefs. Opened on October 9, 1900, the train station's imposing Gothic architecture is similar in design to Washington, D.C.'s historic post office.

Facing page: The current Metro Nashville and Davidson County Courthouse was built in 1937, the fifth building on Nashville's Public Square site. Art Deco in style, the interior was adorned in gold leaf, bronze, marble, and granite to affirm that government stood rock solid even in the middle of the Great Depression.

Above: Light Meander, a sculpture in Nashville's West Riverfront Park, forms a nexus between the Cumberland River and downtown Nashville. The curvilinear form of the sculpture is based on the meanders of the Cumberland River.

Right: The Music City Walk of Fame pays homage to the greats in Nashville's musical history, complementing the Country Music Hall of Fame located across the street.

Facing page: In the center of a mid-town roundabout stands the controversial *Musica*. This monumental bronze of larger-than-life nudes by Nashville's Alan LeQuire is located in the heart of Music Row.

Above: Just over a mile south of Nashville's downtown is Fort Negley Park, an urban greenspace that occupies the Civil War site of Fort Negley. Its visitor center helps interpret one of the Civil War's most important battles. Many of the walls and battlements still stand today.

Left: Two Rivers Greenway starts at Percy Priest Dam, winding along the Stones River to Two Rivers Park, where a pedestrian bridge crosses the Cumberland River and connects to the Shelby Bottoms Greenway.

Far left: Radnor Lake State Park is a 1,332-acre park in Davidson County. It is a favorite destination of Nashvillians for hiking, wildlife viewing, and environmental education programs.

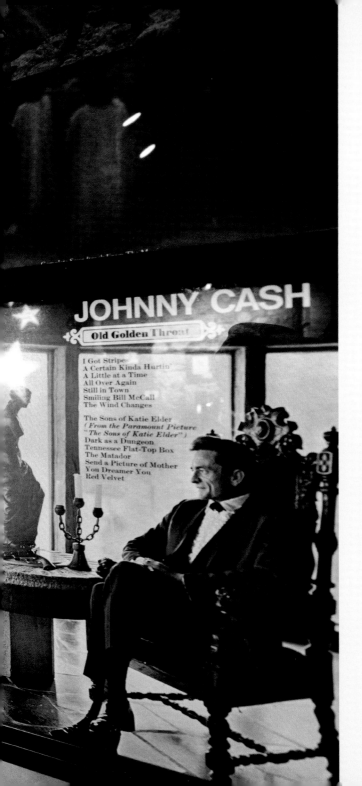

Above: The Johnny Cash Museum provides an in-depth look at the "Man in Black's" amazing life. Featuring hundreds of artifacts and interactive exhibits, it is the most comprehensive collection of Johnny Cash artifacts and memorabilia in the world.

Left: Johnny Cash was one of the most prolific recording artists of his day, with ninety-six albums over a music career spanning forty years.

Above: The Ryman Auditorium has often been referred to as the "Carnegie Hall of the South" because of the many international acts it has brought to Nashville. John Philip Sousa, Harry Houdini, Enrico Caruso, Charlie Chaplin, W. C. Fields, and Bob Hope have all played the hall. In 1943, the Grand Ole Opry radio show moved there, and the musical world would never be the same. Later renovated into a world-class concert hall, the Ryman reopened with a broadcast of *A Prairie Home Companion* in 1994. The Opry moves back to the Ryman during winter months.

Right: The Grand Ole Opry is the longest-running radio broadcast in U.S. history. In 1974 it moved to its current location adjacent to Briley Parkway and Opryland Resort Hotel. The Opry continues to perform here from March through November each year.

BOB SCHATZ

Growing up in Nashville, Bob Schatz's admiration of photography began as a small child. Before he was six, his parents discovered that he had been sneaking his father's camera. A neighbor came to the rescue with a gift of a Brownie box camera for Schatz's eighth birthday. Self-taught throughout his childhood and adolescence, he found the magic of the darkroom when his high school yearbook advisor showed him how to process film and prints. Bob attended Belmont University, where he entered prints in a statewide photography competition his sophomore year. Although he lost first place to a professor at another college, Schatz eagerly pursued his passion throughout his college years. He won "Best in Show" at the Nashville Art Directors Guild by his senior year. His photographs continue to be recognized, winning many regional and national awards.

Schatz's work is frequently seen in print and internet advertising, corporate brochures, annual reports, books, and magazines. His clientele includes *Time* magazine, McMillian Publishing, Honeywell International, HCA, and many others. His artworks have been exhibited around the country and are included in the permanent collections of museums, corporations, and private collectors. Schatz's portfolio can be viewed at www.stockschatz.com, and his blog is at www.bobschatz.com.